Happy Mind, Happy Heart

Written by Carrie Girdler
Illustrated by Laura Elliott

Copyright © 2025 by Carrie Girdler and Alanna Rusnak Publishing

All rights reserved. This book or any portion thereof may not be reproduced or used in any manner whatsoever without the express written permission of the author, except for brief excerpts in a book review or journal.

Elements of the artwork were created using CHATGPT (2025).

ISBN: 978-1-990336-98-0
Contact the publisher for Library and Archives Canada catalogue information.

ALANNA RUSNAK PUBLISHING
Alanna Rusnak Publishing is an imprint of Chicken House Press
chickenhousepress.ca

For Tucker, Maybel and Hutton with the deepest love possible,
Grandma

Welcome, little friend, let's start!

We're going on a journey to a happy heart.

When you feel a little mad,
Or maybe even a little sad,

There's something special you can do,
To bring back the happy you!

First, let's try some deep, deep breaths,
Breathe in like a dragon, and out with a rest.
Take a deep breath, in and out,
Feel the calm all about.

Now, let's play a quiet game,
Mindfulness is its name.

Close your eyes and listen near,

What are the sounds that you can hear?

Birds chirping, the wind's gentle song,
This is where we all belong.

When the world feels big and loud,
Focus on the here and now.

Feel your toes, give a wiggle.
Do you feel a happy giggle?

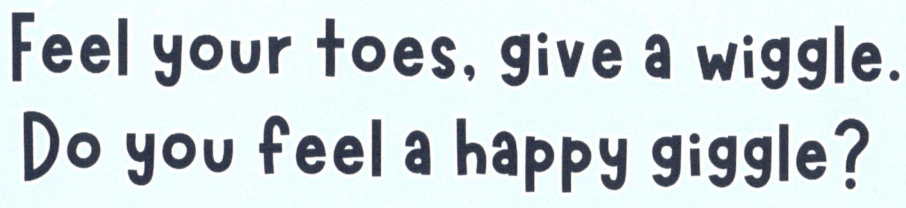

Next, let's practice gratitude,
It's a way to change your mood!

Think of something that makes you glad,
A toy, a friend, or fun you've had.
Say "thank you" with a smile so bright,
Feel your heart fill with light.

When you're thankful for what you've got,
The happy feelings grow a lot.

So remember, when you're feeling blue,
These are some things that you can do.

Happy mind, happy heart,
These are skills that make you smart.
With these tools, you'll always find,
A way to have a peaceful mind.

Good mental health is just as important for children as it is for adults. Creating supportive environments where kids feel safe to express themselves and build healthy coping skills can make all the difference. Here are some easy and enjoyable activities you can try with children to boost their well-being:

1. Go on a Mindful Nature Walk:

Take a walk outside and invite children to use their senses to explore the world around them. Ask questions like, "What can you hear? What can you smell? How does the air feel on your skin?" Nature walks can be a wonderful way to reset and relax.

2. Start a Gratitude Journal:

Encourage children to keep a simple journal where they write or draw something they are grateful for each day. It could be something fun they did, a kindness someone showed them, or even a favourite snack. Talking about gratitude helps kids focus on the good things around them and builds emotional resilience.

3. Check-In and Share Feelings:

Make it a daily habit to ask children how they're feeling using words, drawings, or even a "feelings thermometer" where they can point to a colour that matches their mood. Let them know it's okay to feel sad, mad, or worried and that you are there to listen. You can also practice simple coping strategies together, like deep breathing, counting to ten, or doing a quick silly dance to shake off tough emotions.

4. Encourage Creative Expression:

Provide children with opportunities to express themselves through art, music, storytelling, or imaginative play. Drawing, painting, building, or even making up silly songs can help them process their thoughts and feelings. Celebrate their creativity and encourage them to share their creations if they want to.

By incorporating these activities into daily routines, parents and teachers can help children build emotional resilience and develop healthy ways to manage their feelings. The most important thing is to let kids know they are heard, supported, and loved.

Carrie Girdler lives on a farm outside Walkerton, Ontario, with her husband, Scott. She is a proud mother of three children and grandmother to three beautiful grandchildren. Her family brings joy to her life! With over 28 years of experience in education as a classroom teacher, reading specialist, and elementary principal, Carrie dedicated her career to fostering a love of reading in children. After retiring a year ago, she founded a Nature School on their family farm, embracing her love of the outdoors. In the past year, she also fulfilled a lifelong dream by writing her first children's book, bringing her love of stories to life.

www.ingramcontent.com/pod-product-compliance
Lightning Source LLC
Chambersburg PA
CBHW040031050426
42453CB00002B/84